SUCCESSFUL IRISH BUSINESSMEN

How to be a Successful Irish Businessman

by

MICHAEL KEANE

THE MERCIER PRESS
DUBLIN and CORK

THE MERCIER PRESS,
4 Bridge Street, Cork
25 Lower Abbey Street, Dublin.

ISBN 0 85342 572 8

CONTENTS

How to be a Successful Irish Businessman

If you want to succeed in Irish business get one idea and develop it. Treat this idea like a piece of wood. Whittle away all the other deadwood ideas which will dissipate your energies and decimate your profits and stick to the single track.

A teacher once told me that the four biggest dunces in his class were the four richest men in his part of the country because they had only four ideas among them and they made themselves four fortunes whereas the bright boys, who had as many ideas in their heads as an archer has arrows in his quiver, never seemed to hit a worthwhile target. Like the old woman who lived in the shoe they had so many ideas they did not know what to do with them. They looked at the pros and cons, the ifs and buts, the whys and the wherefores, the maybes and maybe nots until each idea was but a pale ghost of its original and like its ethereal counterpart dissolved into nothingness.

One of the dullards had an idea about turf and he made a fortune out of it after the war when coal was scarce. He bought secondhand army lorries and got first class service from ex-servicemen who were just then hitting the civilian dole queues. In no time he was a millionaire and his entourage of workers became mini-millionaires in their own right.

The next fellow made a fortune out of butter which he sold at a £1 per pound. He could not get enough of it so great was the demand. So, without any great exertion on his part, he became another post-war millionaire. He was a very religious man who attributed his success to the number of pilgrimages he made to Rome and Lourdes. The first time he set out for Lourdes he never got there. He stayed over in Rome because, as he said when he got home, 'Dem Eyetalian wimmen have foine legs'.

The third chap made a fortune out of the grocery business. He started with cigarettes. When they were ten pence halfpenny a packet (old money) he sold five at a time for five pence halfpenny and made one halfpenny profit on every ten. You see, cigarettes were scarce too during the last war and he just could not be handing out tens to people. The bright boys would turn up their noses at such small pickings but our friend had only one idea — to make money slowly but surely.

Next it was the turn of matches. He split each box into two and provided cheap labour for local schoolboys. In those days a halfpenny was good money and for a halfpenny each he got schoolboys to collect the empty boxes. He would not accept them unless they were bone dry. A man of impeccable standards! For another halfpenny each he got them to empty half the matches from fifty boxes into fifty empties (for he was nothing if not generous). So for the expenditure of one penny he made a profit of fifty pennies which was the price of fifty boxes.

Nothing escaped his scythe. Next it was the turn of sweets which — you're quite right — were also scarce. He specialised in sweets which cost ten pence halfpenny per half pound or six pence halfpenny per quarter and never sold anyone more than two ounces for he wanted to give everyone a fair crack of the whip. Again pickings were small — an extra halfpenny on each quarter. Farthings were in use, of course, during this period but it would be a very shortsighted customer who would insist in getting his farthing's worth. His original idea was to make a fortune out of halfpennies and how well he succeeded may be gauged from the fact that he left £50,000 (to his heirs) which in halfpennies of the old kind amounted to 24,000,000. Fair play to him, he was not above overcharging for other commodities as well for,

God be good to him, he was no snob.

Dunce number four made a fortune out of blackthorn. His labour force was recruited from the bums and ne'er-do-wells who idled at street corners. He lured them from their leisure to help him with promises of free porter which they adored and plenty of fresh air which not one of them had the slightest interest in. They scoured the woods and dales of rural Ireland for their raw material and before long your man's blackthorn walking sticks were hopping off the polls of urban Teddy Boys while in Chicago's saloons his blackthorn pipes were creating smoke screens, behind which more than plug was cut. It was only when he denuded the hills and forests of his native Kerry that he stopped making money.

Anyone of the four of them could not pass an exam if it killed him. Where would they be if they had? There were many other not so bright boys (scholastically, that is) who did well. Some made fortunes out of thirst (other people's) and more made fortunes out of 'Ating' houses. Some out of guns and more out of buns. The fellow who made his money out of buns told me that he got his idea while listening to a farmer talking to his son on the morning of an Abbeyfeale calf fair and I quote:

Farmer: 'Will you ate a bun?'

Son: 'Wouldn't I ate a winda fullovum.'

Our friend supplied many windafulls and while

10

the envious may try to crack his plate glass they'll never get near his gold plate.

Others made fortunes out of gallon sweets. There's many a farmer would mow an acre of land after a feed of gallon sweets. Gallon sweets were the making of dentists – a job that's all pull.

I know fellas who made fortunes out of bulls and others who made them out of bulldozers because the poor chaps were not good at their sums.

So, for God's sake, parents, if the kids have just one idea let them be – they could be potential millionaires but if their heads are full of ideas they'll either wind up as civil servants or teachers or hired help of some kind while chappies not half as bright will be making fortunes.

In concluding let me make a few suggestions that you could capitalise on:

1. If you are a plastics merchant start a campaign to bring back collar studs and make yourself a fortune.

2. This is for leprachauns – I know there are a few left who have not emigrated to the U.S. Why not invisibly mend broken cigars and peddle them to third class tourists at half price?

3. You're an entrepreneur. Why not persuade people who are very busy to let you do their Christmas shopping for them. I know, I know, it's a very personal thing but it's worth trying.

There would be a double commission — from the customer and from the shops to whom you would be giving bulk custom.

4. You're a slightly vulgar type and not above making a few bob out of something very low. I speak of the po which lurked under every bed in the Ireland of my youth. Start a campaign to resurrect it and before you know where you are they'll be indispensable as will you, for you'll be the sole Irish distributor.

5. You're a chicken farmer and things are not so good. Right? Feather beds must come back. What good is that to you? I can see the headlines now, 'Feathers fetch more than chicks. Co. Cork farmer breeds long-feathered chicks and makes fortune.'

6. You're a turfman. There are endless ways of making a fortune out of turf and its by-products. One of the easiest ways for a beginner is to wrap up individual sods in green paper and peddle them to coach-touring Americans. You'll make money and you'll get all the turf back if you put your name and address on each package because the Customs people won't allow it out of the country.

7. You're a shamrock grower who is being done by the middle man or woman. Get your own jet fleet and sell direct. You'll get your overheads back in no time and make a fortune besides.

8. You're a collector. Buy a genuine old Irish pigsty and transport it to the U.S. There won't be a pigsty left in this country if it catches on. And you'll make a few thousand grand into the bargain.

9. You're in the tin business. Start a campaign to bring back pipe caps. They are long overdue for revival and the tin industry needs a bit of a boost as does your pocket, so go to it.

10. You're a dissatisfied cop. Baton no good for hard headed hobos of present day? Start your own shillelagh factory when you'll be hailed as a hero and made as a millionaire.

11. How would you like to be the first supplier of steel bras for the Irish Women's Army? Or perhaps you'd prefer to supply sexy shirts to military misses? Start your campaign now because there's a fortune waiting for you.

12. I could go on but my publisher is giving me dirty looks from the wings. Take a leaf out of your own copy book, sez he, and stick to one idea — quit now.

How to Pass an Interview

So you're going up for the interview tomorrow? Well, I have a few words of advice for you.

If you're a bright young thing (female) who'll be facing an all male panel a judicious tugging of the skirt above the knee won't do you any harm — in fact it might do you a lot of good. It'll unsettle them. Better them than you, and it will give you time to think. If you're a tasty dish make their mouths water. Let them feast their eyes on your pulchritude (no, it's not a dirty word — it's just everything you've got really) and give them a mind for the main course. If you are showing leg make sure it hits the chairman's eye when you are about to reply so that he'll forget your answer which will probably be wrong anyway and remember you by the shape, make and curvature of your thigh. This is what's known in the trade as getting a leg in.

Remember that all interview boards have to sit on their benumbed bums for at least seven hours every day listening to all sorts of claptrap. They suffer constantly from indigestion. Give them edible answers. Remember constipation and elimination and make sure you don't hasten your own.

If you say that you spent your holidays in Spain and one of the Board asks you to enumerate the main differences between their way of life and ours and you say, 'No difference,' well, you've been offered a carrot and turned up your nose at it. Your interview is as good as lost.

You'd want to know the job inside out. They won't hang you but you'll hang yourself if you don't know what you're talking about. A few ill chosen words can sell you down the river. So you know something about computers! Right. The board haven't a clue. Here's your chance to make an impression. Your problem is – can you communicate in a few words what you know so well because if you can't you've had it, mate.

Unless he is a personal acquaintance, which is most unlikely and would be most improper, your application form is all the chairman has to judge you by. It is your blueprint for selling yourself. If you fail to impress in the area which you should know so well you will find it difficult to rise above the doubts you may have created in the interviewers' minds about your ability. Do not be a Yes or No man. Do not make the examiners work hard for their information. Remember that their cars may be parked in No Parking areas or that they may have had rows with their wives about the house-keeping money before coming out. Make life easy for them and they will be influenced in your favour.

Be pleasant, well-dressed unless, as already advised, you're a snazzy young thing and then, sister, give it to them straight between the eyes. Don't be cheeky. Take a leaf out of Uriah Heep's notebook and be humble. Let on that you're interested in all sorts of social activities from collecting toilet rolls for the black babies to clipping your pet parrot's claws. Be outgoing and shrug off your accomplishments as a matter of no consequence. You can brighten their day. Don't make it all a drag. If you're looking for a job in the Civil Service, for example, it's not because you think it's a cushy job, with little or no work, endless coffee breaks and oodles of sick leave but because you are interested in public administration. Don't look them in the eye when you say this, you might crumble from over exposure. No, you see the mess the government is making of things and you want to have a hand in it.

Ladies on interview boards, particularly elderly ladies, can be critical of young ladies, so remember the age gap, changing fashions, etc. Never wear slacks unless they are elegant and you balance their eye-catching swishiness with well-manicured finger-nails and a modest blouse and jacket. Be cute.

Watch out for accents. I once knew a fella who, because he thought he was asked, 'What is a Hulon?' tried to give answers thereto. His fevered brain conjured up such diverse answers as:

(a) A high pylon
(b) An expensive nylon
(c) Something to do with the Hudson Bay
(d) A kind of seal
(e) The last of the Huguenots (Where he got this from no one will ever know.)
(f) Something to do with Monsieur Hulot's holiday (I ask you?)
(g) An automatic chain saw and then, as his temperature dropped, descended to such pedestrian answers as,
(h) A unit of heat
and finally
(i) A unit of atomic energy
which reply had the chairman on tenter-hooks as he expected to be sent up by an atomic blast at any moment.

The question was, 'Who was Hugh Lane?' Because the questioner had a northern accent our friend took it to be something completely different. For the rest of the interview he felt about as low as a kierogue's kidney.

Be extremely cautious if you are asked about the Pioneer Total Abstinence Association, for example, and you are a drinker yourself. Don't be trapped into being biased. If it is an erudite question don't try to figure it out, say you don't know. Don't be too introspective. Surface occasionally to meet their eyes or you may find them looking at you as if you were a bowl of blanc mange. Don't give them the opportunity of making a meal out of you.

For Heaven's sake don't start going over all your notes at the last moment because not even the greatest memory man of all times could remember all his notes all at once.

The best thing of all to do before going in is to have a chat with the porter. He has ushered in the winners and losers in countless contests and will have words of wisdom to offer. The price of a pint would not be ill spent for the sound tips you will get. Most post mortems are conducted in his presence so if he prescribes a quick walk around the block take his advice.

As you go in, and before you take your seat, try not to trip over mats, etc. If you get to your seat without having broken your neck you can consider yourself lucky.

Look at their faces. Seek to pierce the facade. Interview boards try to appear to be hard men but it's really because they want to hide their own inadequacies. Search for a sign of weakness — tobacco stains on fingers, an inability to meet your eye, circles under the eyes, porter stains on pull-over and lipstick put on lopsidedly by elderly females.

Some interviewers try to be helpful by making various grimaces but how are you to know that it's not because they're suffering from the itch. If you were not at an interview board you might enjoy these facial contortions, and in retrospect no doubt you will enjoy them reminiscently over a glass of beer but when you are facing them every tic tac signal read correctly makes the difference between backing a winner and a loser

Square Pegs

If a chap is a classical scholar it is almost certain that he will be placed in charge of machinery and if he has a mechanical aptitude he is bound to wind up as a translator of oriental manuscripts if he doesn't go mad first.

In a typical office, rubbing shoulders with one another or merely being surly to each other you will find refugee cattle-jobbers, professional chess players, retired sea captains, stool pigeons (always minding other people's business and never their own), bass guitarists, authors, actors and actresses by the score, trapeze artists, duckers, detectives, dreamers, inspectors of mice, buckpassers, professional gamblers and con men. A lot of present day officials would seem to be more suited to the Professional Golf circuit than to the indoor way of life because they spend an awful lot of time on the links.

Your classical scholar doesn't know one end of a machine from the other but that is of no consequence to the people who appoint him. Looked at from a purely philosophical angle they may reason that even though he knows nothing at first after one day at the racket he will know more than anyone else. His true potential, of course, may never be realised because appointments are made in the same way as a lottery – it's all a lucky dip. Thus, a computer unit crying out for a systems designer could wind up with an absentminded professor. The motto seems to be: Throw him in at the deep end and hope he'll survive. It's only his sanity and the customers' money that you are risking.

You'll get bosses who, because they are too strict with staff, would be better off in charge of a platoon of foot soldiers in the French Foreign Legion. People who are too strict drive others to drink, to malingering, to prevarication and retaliation so that instead of saving an office money they add to its costs in the long term and in addition help to create a very poor climate of industrial relations as present day strikes indicate. Rope is all they need to hang themselves.

Then there is the chap who is too lenient. He wants the easy way out of everything. He is indecisive, ignorant, incompetent and in no time at all he becomes a mat upon which everyone treads with impunity.

Routine jobs which require no imagination and very little brains are breeding grounds for dissatisfaction and its temporary cure – alcohol.

Take a man who has had a sound secondary education, who for five years has followed in the footsteps of Horace and Co. or who has become a disciple of Euclid. He suddenly finds himself in the endless labyrinth of crediting contributions to a member of some scheme or other. Flesh and blood will not stand this for long and the victim will repair to a pub to take the first step on the road to becoming a toper.

I have seen men, elegantly dressed, enter an office in the morning and by midday they had become human sponges, with red faces, who could be found sitting on their bottoms on toilet floors with a baby whiskey in one hand and a shake in the other. All because they were apprenticed to demeaning tasks in the first place. People who are frustrated take their frustrations out on others and instead of being helpful they take delight in causing the other person as many difficulties as possible.

One such person, who had a routine job, acquired the habit of singing the little ditty, 'Mares eat oats and does eat oats and little lambs eat ivy', to the acute annoyance of his colleagues until even the most angelic female turned on him. The Higher-Ups never saw the frustration because they lacked interest and understanding. It was all such a good laugh, really.

The thing to do is to leave all your pretensions and all your idealism hanging in the cloakroom with your coat and scarf, don the garb of the conformist and work all day and every day unquestioningly. Each evening you may, in the physical act of donning your overcoat, resurrect your true self. Like your coat it can become shoddy from wear and tear.

You are an actor who plays the same dreary part year in, year out. Remember this your boss expects you to lay down *your* life for *his* friends. There is no task too demanding, no difficulty too daunting that it will deter him from volunteering your services when at that moment you may have a splitting headache.

Even old ladies have been known to take to the bottle after their daily stint of monotonous drudgery. Long ago they may have sacrificed their youthful ambitions on an indifferent altar to the God of Routine.

However, don't get me wrong. Not all square pegs wind up as alcoholics; most of them merely wind up as incompetents. Their hefty salaries nowadays help to cushion them against the daily insults they are forced to stomach from colleagues who, fortuitously, have found a berth suited to their talents. These fortunate ones are inclined to crow, 'Oh! how clever I am.' It is a wonder they do not succumb from the elation experienced in continually contemplating their own cleverness.

Some square pegs by sheer application make out alright. They may have the potential to play in the Big League but have to content themselves in the minor grade. After a while they become stunted in intellectual growth and it is a pitiful thing to see such a person succumb to the insidious disease of indifference. Still, if one has great will power, pertinacity and application it is possible to make a round peg out of a square one but such a case is the exception rather than the rule.

The Art of Killing Time

Imagine that you are a well-paid official who has just been promoted to a position of authority and you find, after you have spent some time in your new role, that on numerous occasions you have very little to do . . . Have a heart! Believe me, it does happen.

You could, of course, circulate among your colleagues looking for work, volunteering perhaps to take some of their load were it not for the fact that you would arouse such suspicion that you would never again be trusted. People would accuse you of ulterior motives, arse-licking and other sycophantic tendencies and it would be said of you that while superficially it might appear that you were magnanimous in reality you were feathering your own nest by trying to make a good impression on the boss who could not fail to notice, after your efforts, that half your colleagues were unnecessary. Motto: Do not rock the boat or everyone may be lost.

So you are left to your own devices. You

could cultivate the serious expression, the dedicated look, the concentrating brow or the furrowed face but these subterfuges are wasted in the absence of an audience. If you are in a room by yourself you could go mad looking at four walls. So you will be forced to seek solace in the pub or in the bookies. In less time than it takes to wipe your snot you'll find that horsebacking and the gargle are no solutions. Hallucinating with glamour girls is O.K. for a while but it is a dead-end recreation. Nail-biting is an appetising pastime until this supply of protein runs out. Writing reports about some fictitious or imaginary occurrence is an excellent ploy but you have to be in the humour for it.

No, I think you will agree that the best way to prevent yourself going loco is to set out a list of duties and stick to them rigidly. Remember that skilful idling requires determination and grit. You must convince everyone that you are extremely busy. Preparing your list of duties could keep you busy for a week at least and they could be as follows:

9.15:

Arrive at office. Always be punctual so that you can idle more efficiently (or as a wag once said about a colleague, 'he came in early so that he could shelter under the umbrella of his punctuality for the rest of the day').

9.15-9.25:

Read paper, cursorily at this point – save the meat for later on.

9.25-9.30:

Mark the attendance book. A great deal of fun can be had by standing with a red biro poised over the paper as latecomers approach. Their puffing and panting will do your heart good but theirs very little.

9.30:

Proceed to jacks with as many newspapers as possible, or if you feel in a salacious mood, a few bawdy magazines. Should you feel the muse stirring take a wad of paper and half a dozen biros. If you must inscribe the walls of the toilets remember to use a felt pen as biros tend to slip on the moist surfaces. Avoid such unimaginative out pourings as, 'Ireland is crippled by the terror of Black Fascism.' Do not, for the love of Mike, create a racket or you may disturb the form-studying punters – they are worse than a nest of wasps when disturbed. If you are an early morning imbiber remember to take cloves and wear your glasses later – they do not betray as cockeyed glances do. A word of warning about sojourning too long in this Stygian region. As most jacks in offices are of the antedeluvian variety you may perish from exposure. I once knew an inspector who always wore a cap when

proceeding below stairs. He died young as a
result of being caught in a draught without his
headgear.

9.45:

All is peace. The paper rustling has ceased. The
creaking and the obnoxious smells are no more.
You sit in solitary seclusion when all the rest
have gone and contemplate the beautiful water-
colour painting which with such foresight you
had rolled up among your papers so that it
could hang from the door hook to provide
inspiration for your daydreaming.

9.45-10:

Find a vacant corner somewhere to do some physical jerks but make sure you are not observed lest
like Hannibal, you become the object of all eyes.

10-10.10:

Buttress your mind against the rigours of the
day. Prepare yourself mentally and physically
for a fatiguing day of doing nothing.

10.10-10.50:

Set pen to paper to write a fictitious report to
some imaginary superior. Pick a title and convince yourself that it is a serious matter which
has to be on your imaginary superior's table by
11.30. For example, 'Do Branches employ
starving mice to eat old files when incinerator
staffs go on prolonged strike?' or 'Are inspectors
of mice on the increase?'

Draw up a list of the five most obnoxious superiors you ever had and state why you reach your conclusions. Draw up an order of demerit.

Explain in not less than fifteen pages why your mind goes blank at the sight of blotting paper.

10.50-11:

Leave the scripts and go for a brisk walk to get away from it all. Avoid the big boss. You may have nothing to do but you are not entitled to walk around as if you had nothing to do.

11-11.30:

Official Coffee break. This may be spent doing:

1. Crosswords
2. Calculating income tax
3. Dreaming about money
4. Worrying about the seniority list for promotion
5. Nail-biting — a delectable and nutritious pastime.

11.30-12:

Have you written to your grannie lately? If not, now's the time and remember there's plenty of it.

12-12.30:

Visit various colleagues before lunch and waste their time. They would waste yours if the thought had occurred to them.

12.30-12.45:

Write a brief description of those who may have been annoyed by your visit, with appropriate comments.

12.45-2.15:

Take a long lunch but do not partake of more than three pints or you may sleep for the afternoon and betray your bibulous inclinations by your loud snores.

2.15-3:

Back to the grind of idling. A long difficult period up to the next coffee break. Such breaks are like oases in the desert in which those who live off their intellectual humps sojourn. Men and women have to be made of steel to last from two to four without a break, the men with their tongues hanging out for a pint and the girls itching to get their hands on their knitting needles. If you are of a literary bent you could try a short story or do the Cryptic crossword in one of the dailies and if you are carrying excess avoirdupois and are over forty you could do worse than making your will. So you're a frustrated old lady; well, why not think of a sophisticated way of murdering your boss.

3-4:

The dark hour of the soul. Adjourn to jacks again. Beware of falling asleep as you may slip off seat and fracture your boondoon or failing that you may sleep beyond five-thirty and be unable to claim overtime for the added period. If you are a gambler now's the time to slip out and check on your wagers, snatch a quick pint or do the shopping.

4.-4.30:

Evening coffee break. This is an excellent time to calculate what you will be getting after income tax deductions as a result of a recent payrise or you could draw up a budget in which you would be able to save thousands on paper and damn all in practice.

4.30-5.30:

Make elaborate plans on how to spend your hardwon freedom when you get off. Try not to trample on old ladies as you stampede out of the building.

I once heard of a chap who was so averse to work that he spent the day walking about. His technique was to pick up a piece of paper and with a concerned expression tap said paper against his teeth as, shaking his head deprecatingly from side to side, he proceeded from room to room, seeking some elusive destination. The only clerical work he did was before an exam when he studied like mad and got paid for it.

In conclusion may I say that the art of opening a file with a blank page and looking at it as if it were filled with the greatest prose on earth is a consummate skill which only comes from long years of practice. Another concept of this art is writing absolutely nothing while going through the motions of writing reams, like a hovercraft flying over the paper. When one is making wiggles and squiggles one should have a steely look in the eyes, with jaw jutting out firmly as if one had just been commissioned and were engaged in translating the Koran into Modern Jazz.

Pipe Smokers

Pipe smokers are on the increase since the cigarette-smoking and cancer scare first surfaced. Formerly in offices one espied thin spirals of smoke but nowadays rooms are filled with dense clouds and the unmistakeable smell of shag.

Smoking a pipe is a leisurely practice, almost a fetish. It has to be executed with care and precision to ensure a satisfactory final outcome.

Pipe-smoking requires patience and the proper equipment. A penknife with a fine blade is an essential for cutting hardpacked tobacco. A packet of fibre pull-throughs is another. Cutting the plug and breaking the sections down into a finer pulp by pressing between the palms is a consummate skill. The accoutrements of one's calling should be scattered about one's desk at convenient points so that each implement necessary to the particular phase of the pre-smoking ritual can be picked up easily.

The regular pipe-smoker will arrange a sheet of blotting paper on his desk. I have known fastidious pipe-smokers who pinned this rectangle down at its four corners with drawing pins to ensure anchorage. A harder piece of cardboard, rectangular in shape, may be placed thereon for use as a tobacco-chopping block anon. The penknife is opened and placed at a convenient angle. The smoker runs his finger lovingly along the blade to test its mettle and if he is an old hand who is not satisfied with its sharpness he may resurrect a steel file or a whetstone to renew its keeness.

Of course, at this point one may ask how can a chap spend all this time on his pipe in the middle of his working day. Well, since patience is the name of the game, he may control his desire for a smoke by deferring this ritual until his coffee break and should the pleasurable exercise then overflow into ordinary working time it would, at the most, only involve a few minutes. However, I have known chaps who had no sooner placed their morning paper to one side than they began to prepare for a smoke. One could observe the boss, from his conning tower, view the performance with misgiving as he constantly checked his watch. He could have saved himself such facial remonstrances if he knew how lost in his cocoon of smoke the smoker was.

The pipe-smoking clerk feels as secure as a bug in a rug within his nimbus. The art of lighting a pipe the long way round acts as a perfect foil against interruptors. Fumes are really the best thing to make others fume. One can reduce a fussy caller to a spluttering nuisance and one can frustrate those robots, practising the cult of the impersonal, who must have instant attention. There is something very soothing in biting into the stem of a curved consoler as if indeed it were the hard neck of the fuming colleague who believes that the office would come apart at the seams without his constant efforts on its behalf. The fussy caller may prance, dance or expostulate to no avail for a good pipe-smoker always keeps his cool and behind his ephemeral curtain he gains anxious moments in which to plan his defence.

However, time to continue with the smoking ritual. Stem cleaners, in their wiry fibre off-whiteness, are laid out. The plug is unwrapped and made ready for the cutting. The pipe is dismantled with the stem on the left and the bowl on the right (if it is an old-fashioned pipe). The bowl is scraped clean and the blackened ashes are tipped out on to a corner of the rectangle of blotting paper. The stem portion is placed in the mouth. The smokers grips firmly with his teeth and blows through the hole in the stem. If he is not satisfied he selects one of the fibres and begins to pull it through the orifice in the stem in order to clear that passage of tar.

When this is done he blows through the orifice

again and if satisfied he rejoins the stem to the bowl and blows through tentatively taking no notice of the long queue of nail-biting officials building up in the wings. Iron will-power, boy, that's what you need and an ability to avoid meeting their eye otherwise you will be pinned down by the most inexorable staple there is — the common stare.

He then takes his penknife and begins to cut slim curling strips off the plug. Next he works these strips between his palms, grinding them into pulp which he then begins to pack into the bowl with a steel packer. When this is done, much to the relief of those dodgers who have remained in the queue in preference to returning to work, he is ready to light up, paying no heed to the cranky auld one who threatens him with her umbrella.

Pipe-smokers, fifty years ago, boasted a filigreed metal cap which they kept taking off and putting on much like the way an Indian used a blanket to make smoke signals. A 'redden' for the pipe was a great thing then. The best thing about these old steel caps was that they were like miniature ovens for transporting portion of the redhot coal prior to placing it atop of the packed shag in the bowl. This further act in the ritual has now been scrapped due, I think, to the numerous novenas offered up by bosses as much as to the changing times and the introduction of fast-filling pipes.

The expression on a pipe-smoker's face after taking his first puff cannot be unlike that which graced the Deity's on his first beholding the finished globe of the earth. Interrupting a pipe-smoker at this point is as dangerous as entering a she-bear's den when she fondles her first cub.

These first pulls are sheer ecstacy. After them a pipe-smoker is game for anything, even for work. The more contented the expression on his face the more discontented becomes that on everyone else's face for his heaven is their hell. Like the volcano he showers molten fumes upon the populace but remains aloof from it all himself and when the clouds recede he has the further prospective pleasure of cleaning and replacing his accoutrements at which task he should be able to waste at least another fifteen minutes.

His colleagues' reaction to the fall-out is to let him know by a barrage of coughing (to which he is impervious at this stage) that his enjoyment is their enslavement.

The pipe-smoker dwells in an enchanted land where there are no clouds. He can be brought back to earth by a blast of fresh air when an irate colleague maliciously opens a window. Fresh air has the same effect on a pipe-smoker as fire has on witch. His smoke screen will be dissipated until he is at the mercy of his fellows who seek to lure him back by intricate questioning into the jungle of official jargon.

So the clouds drift ceilingwards or through slightly opened windows while the boss calculates that almost an hour of official time has been wasted between the preparation, the enjoyment and the replacement of this man's pipe to say nothing of the numerous officials who have been rendered hors de combat. And always in the back of his mind is the knowledge that the dissipation of smoke is but temporary and that when the fancy takes him the pipe-smoker will be building his smoke screen again.

The Grille Technique

(A subterfuge for officials who
do not want to be disturbed)

The ostrich sticks its head in the sand. There is very little sand in large offices but there is a more simple expedient. You may rest your elbows on your desk and support your head by placing the thumbs of the right and left hands under your jaw. The palms and fingers may act as blinkers or winkers. While the fingers remain closed you cannot see to the left or to the right. However, if you realise that your fingers are a grille which may be opened or closed at your own whim or as exigency demands you may appear to be engrossed in your work while you are, in fact, hallucinating with a delectable Goddess on the sunny side of Mount Olympus.

The ostrich needs only an open space in the desert. The clerical worker, to effect his withdrawal from reality, has to surround himself on at least three sides with impenetrable foliage.

First of all, you must so position your desk as to allow for only one approach from the right. Surround yourself with a tri-lateral defensive system of pigeonholes stretching from floor to ceiling. Ensure that the distance between the back of your chair and the pigeonholes at your rear is so minute that it will not permit the passage of even the most tenuous person. Push your desk right up against the wall or window on your left so that no one can reach you from that side and if another person faces you ensure that it is impossible for any interloper to squeeze behind him/her in order to annoy you from the front. The impregnability of this position will only be achieved after endless rearrangements, readjustments and realignments. If the approaches to your desk are barricaded on three sides it follows that all approaches must be made from the remaining side which is the right in your case. From behind the grille of your fingers you may screen your callers without appearing to do so.

It is quite exciting in a sort of dispassionate way to observe a queue elongate in order to see you — somewhat like a queue of cars waiting for a car ferry. There is no guarantee that all or indeed any of your queue will ever reach you. Your defensive system and the grille technique has been designed to break the spirit of even the most patient. Other potential callers can be put off by the mere sight of a queue. To be successful you must be ice-cool. Softheartedness is fatal.

In the summertime when the sun blazes down

(where?) and torpor descends on mortal men in the siesta period those who are bored, fat or middle-aged will feel an irresistible urge to sleep. If you belong to one of these categories naturally you will try to shrug it off at first lest, in succumbing, you may by uncontrollable speech reveal your animosity towards the boss or your prejudice towards your colleagues. When sleep is inevitable you must employ the grille technique otherwise you are particularly vunerable as you sit slumped in your seat with your head resting on your hands.

Post prandial naps have their own special ritual. The square of blotting paper, garlanded with the wiggles and squiggles of experimental calligraphy, which reposes on the desk of every clerk, has to be adjusted into a strictly rectangular position. A file of papers is then opened and placed to the left of the sitter. The pipe is taken out and placed, stem foremost, in the concave slot of an ashtray. A half-opened box of matches, slightly tilted, is placed beside it. One lowers one's head to rest between the span of thumb and forefingers and at this juncture, one may allow a sigh of contentment to escape as one settles down to snooze behind the grille of the fingers.

Nappers of this sort are only half asleep. They float between two worlds and some who are on the verge of sleep experience a sensation similar to that of a fowler as he waits under cover for the first duck to appear.

If there happens to be a creaking board amongst the flooring on your right it will help you to develop a high audio-frequency as anyone stepping on it will instantly cause a reaction to trigger off in the innermost recesses of your brain. If the caller approaches quickly there should be no sign of emotion in the bent head. When you become aware of the presence of an intruder you should not immediately open your eyes. You should hold your breath, listening intently and sniffing imperceptibly for a tell-tale aroma. The fingers should only open by the most infinitesimal fraction, a maneouvre so perfectly executed as to be invisible to the most observant onlooker. Your awareness of another's presence should not be betrayed by even the merest flicker of an eyelash. Once the grille has closed on silent hinges you can open your eyes in the certain knowledge that this action will not be visible to the person on the other side. Part your lips slightly, if you like, and allow your hand like a crab's feeler to edge inch by stealthy inch towards the file of papers until it rests on the open page. Again you may open the grille ever so slightly to steal a surreptitious glance sideways to study the shape, make and calibre of your fretting caller. (If he gets too close you will only be able to view him amidships and everyone looks the same thereabouts).

If, in an official sense, your visitor is a person of no consequence — a minor clerk or a messenger — there should be no immediate change in your disposition but if it is a superior who is pawing the ground like a young stallion you should go through an elaborate quick-change routine, closing the grille slowly again, flicking by a page of the file with your left hand, removing your right hand support from under your chin, reaching for your pipe and placing the stem between your teeth. Only when you reach for the matches should you surface and notice your caller for the first time, by the ways, affording yourself the luxury of stuttering in surprise, 'My Goodness — eh-eh-eh we-we-we-were you waiting long? I-I-I'm afraid I-I was so absorbed in this file that-that-that I never no-no-noticed you.' The word 'absorb' will really get him be he a cynic or a true believer.

If the great man is a cynic he'll know you staged it all, of course. He will be madly jealous and rush off, without molesting you, in order to try the same technique on his own superior. But if he is an unsuspecting sort he'll be full of apology for disturbing you and rest assured that your name will figure high in the list he next considers for promotion. He'll be thinking such thoughts as, 'Studious chap. Great concentration. Absorbed in his work. Shows great zeal, etc., etc., etc.'

If he is an impressionable sort he cannot but

admire your technique.   You're next door to a
genius.

Yes, I can unreservedly recommend the grille as
the most inexpensive security device on the market.

Getting a Good
Second - In -Command

In any sphere of activity a good second-in-command is worth his weight in gold. It's easy enough to get a second-in-command but to get a good one — that's a horse of a different colour. Once you find such a rare bird you'll be made for life.

He will cushion you against the assaults of an unappreciative public, against a demanding staff who can be like suckling pigs in their desire for the money teat, against your superiors who are forever requesting data and output and greater efficiency and higher sales or what have you. All of these you would be unable to supply in his absence. He relieves you of all that sort of jazz. With such a stand-in, and your good second-in-command need not necessarily be a man, you may be officially in your office at your desk and unofficially at a variety of places:-

(a) A golf course if you chase after the small ball
(b) A pub if you want to escape from it all
(c) An Art Gallery if you want to improve your mind

(d) With a blonde in your chosen retreat if you are a dallier with the ladies or

(e) In a bookies' joint if you fancy losing a fortune.

A good second-in-command should be like a sluice gate, only allowing the merest trickle of correspondence to reach you so that you may make considered judgments on weighty topics without being bothered by a wealth of trivia.

If you are a boss you should sit as far back from the door as possible and site second-in-command in a position of prominence, not unlike that of the Statue of Liberty, so that all visiting craft cannot fail to see him. Try to remain unobstrusive and if you cannot get a screen you should shore up with a rampart of files or whatever it is that you do business in to preserve yourself from those insidious creatures who are forever ferretting out information.

Let S-I-C do all the barking but you should only bite when you have to. You should try and be popular with all and sundry and blame him for any inconvenience caused or unpopular decisions arrived at.

Of course, don't forget to throw your trusty watchdog an occasional bone of flattery. You could also stand him an odd pint or allow him to stand you one. You might do worse than buy a book of Kerry jokes and feed him the choicest morsels, having first ascertained that he's not a Kerryman. Find out what his hobbies are — reading, fishing, football, visiting ancient monuments, poteen making or viewing mini-skirts (if there are any left) — and display a great interest. This will warm him towards you.

Ask him about his relations. Find out if he has any eminent brothers, sisters or relatives, whether he is proud or jealous of them and sympathise or enthuse as you see fit.

If he is a young man be sympathetic to his problems. It he is married and paying for a house or trying to raise a family on the lowest point of his salary scale lend a fatherly ear. If, on the other hand, he is middle-aged and beginning to feel his stomach muscles sag give him an occasional build up to boost his ego. Say you understand, etc., etc., nodding your head wisely and making deprecating sounds in your throat. Give him an odd buckshee half day, having ensured in advance that nothing of a controversial nature, which could land you in the soup, is likely to surface that afternoon.

Make sure he does not sit in a draught for if he catches cold and stays out sick you will be stuck with all his work and there will be no one to protect you from those who, because of your excellent camouflage, will have been unaware of your existence up to then. Suffer him to be a trifle late in the mornings occasionally if it prevents him from trying to beat the lights and turning himself into a corpus delicti. He might just as well run the car over you. Preserve him as if he were a jar of youth elixir.

Admittedly there are his annual holidays the one fly in the ointment. You should start limbering up about three weeks before these are due to commence and increase your workouts to a more intensive kind for the final two weeks otherwise you are liable to sustain a fierce heart attack when the floodgates open and the volume hits you in his absence. Be a constant visitor to your Local Health Food store for advice and sustenance. Go for long walks and breathe deeply. Try to refrain from cursing. Be prepared for an unpleasant time and say a prayer that his holidays will pass quickly, that he will be blessed with fine weather and that he will get a gorgeous tan.

When he returns don't get sentimental about his work which you have been doing in his absence. Pile it all back on him and advise telephone callers and interruptors that S-I-C deals with whatever it is they are enquiring about. He'll be a glutton for work after his long lay-off but volunteer to help as if you enjoyed that sort of caper. You're certain to get a negative for above all he wishes to impress and he'll be raring to get rid of his surplus energy after lolling on the hot sands. He may have got a little reckless with freedom so don't be too finicky with his draft letters, particularly if he fancies himself as a scribe having penned pointed sayings on holiday postcards. Give him a few days to settle and listen open-mouthed to his little store of holiday reminiscences. Before you know where you are you'll be having your fifty week all-the-year-round holiday once again.

Pray against the day when someone may recognise his ability because one of the risks of over-exposing him is that you may fix him more firmly in the big boss's eye. When an interview comes round the big man may want to send him further, not having your vested interest, and you may go through the long purgatory of waiting for another good second-in-command. *Believe me, it only happens once in a lifetime.*

Health Fanatics

With such an accent on the incidence of heart disease, lung cancer and arthritis at the present time the health fanatics have become an absolute menace. They take their role in life so seriously that if some health scribe whom they have never heard of before advised them to eat buttercups they would do so with the greatest relish. They get so enthusiastic about exercises, open windows, deep breathing, Transcendental Meditation, fruit juices, fly-swatting and mice cremation that they want to involve everyone else in their fanaticism.

Morning time for the health fanatic commences with tongue scansion and if that organ happens to be discoloured it will worry him for the whole day. Every time he feels a pinch or a spasm of wind or an answering twitch to his nervous anticipation thereof he will refer to the crystal ball of his tongue. The depth and variety of its discolouration will determine the extent of his worry. He will listen with avid ears to hear someone say that they have a serious ailment in order to be able to

chime in and say, 'I have that too,' being unsporting enough to rob the person of his moment
of excruciating agony. A sensible woman once
told me that nearly all aches and pains experienced
in middle age are caused by *wind,* as a result of
eating too fast or not at all. The wind pains are
easily recognisable by the sensible person but to
the health fanatic they are the harbingers of heart
attacks, cancer of the colon, ulcers and gall stones.
You name it, he worries about it.

Health fanatics go about glaring at smokers or
coughing incessantly in their presence. Smokers
ignore them or offer them some fatherly advice:
'You'd want to look after that auld cough.' Armed
with ruler or duster they prowl about the corridors
of large office blocks seeking for those flies who
have escaped fly paper and spider. They are
dedicated people with faces as sharp as razor blades
and horizons as boundless as curved ceilings.
Female health fanatics go mad at the sight of a
mouse as if his very presence were going to start a
pestilence. Inspectors of mice are on the increase
to deal with these diminutive buckos. Health
fanatics wash their hands before and after meals
and about a hundred other times per day on the
slightest provocation. Their heads are never still,
always swivelling for fear of an onslaught by one
of the best small aircraft in existence, the common
fly, and for fear of excremental attack by seagull

and pigeon.

In shops they glare at assistants who unhygienically handle meat or what have you - their life is one long glare. They are afraid of cracked cups, nail biters, cigarette and pipe smokers, spitters, sneezers, open windows, kierogues and cobwebs.

Your health fanatic is a perpetual seeker out who could easily be mistaken for a spy or a Peeping Tom and castigated therefor. They have the curiosity of cats and the tact of trumpetting elephants. They are forever wagging fingers or remonstrating with minors when not engaged in gulping fresh air.

I once knew a potential health fanatic who used to say to his boss, 'Could I possibly get off early to do an urgent message?' or some other similar excuse. Said boss would be proceeding home in a bus when he would behold an astonishing spectacle on the pavement, a man with flailing, windmilling arms taking giant strides and breathing deep breaths of exhaust fumes, none other than – uh-huh! you guessed it – our friend who asked to get off early. Acting on the advice of health scribes again. The only one to benefit from this walk would be the local undertaker.

The desk drawers of health fanatics are crammed full of medical journals and health magazines which they devour with the same avidity as the salacious reader does dirty stories. When they see their favourite diseases mentioned they go into a sort of orgasm from the sheer joy of it all.

Health fanatics are forever clearing cobwebs from ancient ceilings little realising that they could precipitate an avalanche of crumbling plaster or disrupt the endlessly expanding network so intricately woven by spiders to collaborate in trapping their own arch enemy.

I once knew a wag who twisted the little advice notices placed on toilet walls by these fanatical hopefuls. A tag such as 'please don't throw cigarette butts into the urinals,' would be extended to, 'as they are too soggy to smoke afterwards.'

During dinner hour health fanatics are to be observed going about offices opening windows. Some go the whole hog, almost yanking the window out of its moorings, others surreptitiously raising the sashes only a fraction of an inch with the result that the person sitting next to them will, while experiencing an unmerciful draught in the afternoon, be unable to determine its source.

Once as a result of the efforts of an elderly female health fanatic a batch of postal orders was blown out through the top window of an office block and as the Chief Executive returned from lunch one of them, impelled by wind-driven rain, smacked him right in the kisser, to his official incredulity and personal consternation.

Health fanatics are to be observed in secret

corners practising arm swings and toe touching in the belief that they are adding years to their life. They must be forever on guard lest some tiny four-footed interloper steal a march on them.

A health fanatic of my acquaintance was wont to take his holidays in late autumn, the better to protect himself against the approaching winter. On a number of occasions he surprised everyone, including himself, by being the first to succumb to the flu. Health is not purchased by adherence to a set of rules and regulations.

I once knew a health fanatic who was convinced that he had two heart beats. The cause was quite simple. While he was asleep in his digs a new boarder was ushered into his room. This man removed his watch and was about to unrobe when the landlady returned to tell him that she had another berth for him upstairs. In his hurry he left his turnip of a watch on the dressing table. Our friend woke up in the middle of the night to hear his heart and, as he thought, its twin reverberation, the thump of the watch which was removed in the morning before he awoke, leaving him with the legacy of two heartbeats. I suppose two heart beats are better than none.

Health fanatics are to be pitied for they are endlessly on the Qui Vive — better for them to break all the daft rules and live to the ripe old age of ninety in the process.

The Art of
letting on to be mad

If you do not care for work, like to sleep during the day and cannot make even the simplest decision the thing for you to do is to let on to be mad.

First of all you must decide on a particular form of madness and stick to it. Then, allow yourself a period of rehearsal — say, a month — before you try it out on the boss. Begin in a low key and gradually increase the tempo of your madness. If you go completely overboard all at once you may drive him mad too and no office or business can afford two mad people at the one time.

Secondly, you should cultivate a form of madness which would be the least likely to do you any permanent damage. In other words you should bring all your sanity to bear in creating a credible form of insanity. For after all, what is the point in letting on to be mad if one cannot enjoy one's madness.

Thirdly, you should test out your madness on a genuine nutcase. If you frighten a real madman sane people won't have a chance and will be most anxious to give you a wide berth in the future.

If you are a civil servant, for example, there is no fear of you losing your job. You are in for life so you might as well enjoy it. Remember your madness need only be a nine to five one. You can compensate with an after-work sanity.

You might reflect on just one advantage. Take payday for instance when others are shelling out to collectors and ticket sellers you will have acquired complete immunity because, for example, of the ferocious roar with which you greet interlopers or because of the numerous black eyes which bear evidence to your unerring accuracy with the mitts or for whatsoever it is you have earned a reputation.

I once knew a lady who used to let out such an unmerciful screech at her boss that he would scurry backwards to his burrow like a frightened rabbit. She would then make remarks which hit amazingly close to the bone of the gentleman on the receiving end. After a while she became the envy of all those who had thought of going mad themselves. Now she was in heaven, cashing in on her great idea while they were still in purgatory, seeking a remission for their sanity.

To preserve the heaven of her new found bliss she was obliged to observe certain rites and rituals. She never spoke to anyone and did not answer telephones. If her boss communicated with her she made King Kong-like rumblings which he, poor slob, could not interpret. Could you? Consequently, as a progressive member of his staff she was a dead loss.

Dress is very important if you want to present a character of madness. The odder the better. For a lady, a long red silken hose on her left leg contrasts vividly with a bottle green cheap nylon at half mast on her right. A skeleton umbrella is also excellent on a wet day because if you were sensible enough to be able to protect yourself from the rain you would fool nobody.

Lipstick and powder also play very important roles particularly if they are misapplied. Lipstick should be used above or below the lips, never on them. An extra pair of lips, painted lopsidedly on the cheeks, is a decided asset. People may stare and laugh but what matter if immunity from official duties is the prize. And as for callers, admonishingly wagging fingers and cranium tapping by your colleagues direct the footsteps of those who would annoy you elsewhere.

Similarly with outlandish hairstyles. If you are a man you could do worse than cultivate the hairstyle of the Mohawk Indians or one of Ireland's black fascists.

Another middle-aged lady of my acquaintance developed a shocking technique. With the skilful application of make-up she made herself look like one of the walking dead. Her sane colleagues thought she was frightfully daring but then, they reasoned, the poor dear was mad, really mad, otherwise she would never say the things she did to middle-aged gentlemen: 'Take me to bed, darling.' Most guys would oblige if she was a good-looking chick but one look at the zombie face would make them take off like a well-directed golf ball.

Some pseudo madmen of my acquaintance who got blind, maggoty, footless drunk, moryah, said things to their boss which would lead to their instant dismissal if he knew they were of sound mind.

Then, there were those gents whose insanity erupted each morning before the pubs opened. They would stride out of work at ten-thirty and not be seen again until after the 'Holy Hour' in the evenings. For the remainder of the day they engaged in strenuous argument with their familiars.

Then you had the religiously mad — one such person used to go about selling toilet rolls for black babies. Another was wont to spend the day praying aloud, thumping her breast with the regularity of a big drummer at an Orange parade.

I once knew a porter who talked to an Aperture. He never did so until he was certain he was being observed and then he laid it on thick — getting into violent political argument with whoever it was he imagined he saw in the Aperture. Higher ups hurried to the opposite end of the corridor when he approached.

So if you want to avoid responsibility let on that you are a complete nut. You will get an easy job and no one will ever bother you. Should they do so, for any reason, you can assault them without fear of the consequences.

Jealous people may say that you are *not* mad or that, if you are, you are mad the right way. Pay no heed. They seek to lure you from your seclusion. They are eaten up with envy because you thought of it first.

Remember you have to be *daring* and you have to be *original* to be successful.

Finally, here is a set of maxims which every potential pseudo mad man or woman should be familiar with:

(a) Wear glasses with one of the monocles missing and the other one cracked.

(b) Talk to yourself incessantly and occasionally utter outrageously dirty words.

(c) Wear odd sock, shoes, etc.

(d) Carry faded flowers regardless of your sex.

(e) If you are old wear garments suitable to teenagers.

(f) If you are young (and if you are genuine about letting on to be mad you cannot start young enough) wear your grannie's or granda's cast-offs.

(g) Surround yourself with cats, call them Christian names and refer to them as if they were human.

(h) If you are an elderly lady it is a very good ploy to let out an unmerciful ullagon when there is absolute silence. This is very beneficial for everybody because it keeps higher-ups on their toes and wakes those who have already gone to sleep and, consequently, in the long term, repays your employer for your own inefficiency.

Buckpassers

If there is one thing uppermost in the mind of a buckpasser it is that if he can avoid dealing with anything he will do so. A fellow who is averse to work seeks out a victim, usually a myopic fellow who will surface to behold a big man with an inch and a half of ash teetering on the end of his cigarette. The big man throws a document on the table and fallguy picks it up and peers at it. After scanning four pages he looks up to question his visitor only to discover that said worthy has disappeared . . . We will observe a minute's silence, please. Another buckpasser has just passed his buck.

I once knew an inspector who had about 500 files of correspondence on hands before going on holidays. In order to depart with a clean slate, so to speak, he sent the lot of them to another inspector, penning the phrase, 'For you, please,' in each file. The recipient was raging because they were not for him but, for the time being at least, the other man had passed the buck.

Take another man who has a fairly bulky file of correspondence in front of him for weeks on end. Instead of dealing with it he spends his time making wiggles and squiggles on a sheet of blotting paper. He is loathe to leave this pastime for the purpose of saying 'yes,' or 'no.'

Apropos of wiggles and squiggles a weather forecaster once told me of a met man in Montana who doodled quite a lot on his weather chart. On one such occasion his boss rushed into his room and grabbed the chart before our friend could prevent him. As he left he kept mumbling, 'hurricane approaching rapidly from the southwest — evacuate all personnel.' The doodler, having failed to recover his handiwork, got down on his knees and prayed for a hurricane. His prayers were answered by the message that a hurricane was approaching but from the opposite direction to that indicated by his doodling. Subsequently he was suspended by his boss for writing upside down on his weather chart.

From hurricanes to buckpassers. The phrase, 'Not for me, please,' is a familiar refrain which the buckpasser loves to repeat. The buckpasser, who is essentially a non-worker, may receive a missive in the post about which he hasn't got a clue. He will get rid of it as quickly as possible, picking the person who is the least likely to send it back in a hurry — 'For you, please,' — omitting, at the same time, to append his name or initials so that the recipient, even if he felt so inclined, would be unable to return it until he had painstakingly traced the sender by handwriting comparisons and it might be just as quick to deal with the damn thing as do that. More often than not, however, recipients hasten to pass the buck further and a chain reaction sets in.

The born buckpasser forgets altogether about the contents of the letter he seeks to be rid of and about the consequences of his action. It may be a letter or a memo which requires a reply in a matter of days and he, instead of complying, attempts to bury it in the Limbo of lost epistles. Or it may be a letter which, first of all, requires an acknowledgment and a pledge perhaps of further future positive steps to finalise the query. Such an initiative would satisfy the writer at this point in the proceedings but the buckpasser, in his efforts to be rid of it at any price, fails to grasp this simple truth and so, when the question becomes red hot in a few days hence, a scapegoat must be sought in order to spare the blushes of his superiors. Computers have been a Godsend to buckpassers who blame them for everything, knowing that they cannot answer back.

Now we come to the absentminded clerk who issues a letter which requires a reply without remembering to quote the address of his own particular section or sub section so that, in fact, the reply is addressed to a department at large. Such letters wind up in registries where post is sorted and the officer-in-charge sends them to where he/she thinks they should be going with the hopeful tag, 'For you, please'.

Days later they arrive back in the registry with the number of 'Not for me, pleases,' literally running into hundreds. The poor registrar will be demented as will those unfortunate souls to whom she hopefully sends them.

Tension will build up, time will be wasted, and the absent-minded oaf who caused all the confusion will be wondering why people take such a long time to reply to a perfectly straight forward epistle. When blood pressures run high after frustrating searches for documents or previous correspondence to which these missives might refer people who did not realise they were buckpassers will discover that they are after all as they hasten to get rid of the embarrasing correspondence.

Or it may be some obscure regulation or some decision which could be affected by it which lands on the buckpasser's table. His first reaction, on seeing it, is to reach for his pills but on reflection it is much simpler to drop it on a colleague's desk, preferably a conscientious type who is not a buckpasser or someone who has just departed on annual leave so that it will be in a state of suspended animation until he returns when the poor man will get such a shock that all the good of his holiday will disappear instantly.

When a buckpasser passes his buck he experiences a sensation somewhat similar to that of a hen when she lays an egg. Thereafter he has to be on his guard lest some unsporting colleagues seek to return the compliment. It is a time for ground hurlers and first time strikers although frequently it can be more strategic to lob the ball on to the feet of a colleague who can score direct from play.

In the buckpasser business one has to be an accomplished liar. When some higher-up is trying to trace a guilty party one has to act the innocent. Nothing wounds the pride of a buckpasser more than being caught in the act of passing or having a pass traced back to him.

A professional buckpasser who fails to pass his buck will spend hours seeking loopholes and escape clauses without realising that he would be much better employed dealing with the subject from which he wished to escape.

Keep your eye on a buckpasser's hands for in appearing to listen attentively to the most inane jokes he may be passing his buck right under your very nose. The success of his art depends on the foibles of his fellows and like the skilled three card trick man he is very hard to detect.

How to 'Cod' your Boss

There is endless opportunity for an official with an inventive mind to 'cod' his/her boss regarding sick leave or indeed to 'cod' the doctor. A myth circulates amongst members of the public that there is an inexhaustible supply of deputies to take over his duties when he is ill but in practice it is the poor old slob of a boss who has to shoulder the burden. Boss, how are you? Slave, would be nearer the mark.

Perhaps a chap is not feeling up to scratch. He reaches for his medical dictionary (an item no professional malingerer should be without) and falls in love with its description of a particular ailment. There are such marvellous names to choose from. How about the following: Calculus, cellulitis, colitis, diplopia, diverticulitis, hallucination, hysteria and hypertension. Can you imagine the consternation a boss will feel when he opens a letter containing a medical certificate to describe such conditions? He will start soul searching straight away lest he could in any way have been responsible for bringing things to such a pretty pass.

I believe that the commonest disease prevalent amongst young gentlemen in need of a cure on Monday mornings is hardupness. It is always accompanied by a great thirst and may be mistaken for a sore throat but has never yet failed to respond to large injections of capital.

Girls in flats and hostels tend to suffer from anaemia because they spend more money on clothes than on the frames which they enhance. Style is hard to resist. As a result of inadequate diet young ladies disappoint when they are most needed. They are not able for the flu and fall by the wayside. Men tend to suffer from laziness on occasion or they may get browned off from a particular job which creates a desire to escape from it all by going to the races or on a bender.

And if dentists had to deal with all the people who get off early to go to them they would be working night and day. A person may ask to get off to go to the dentist when in fact he is going to the dogs or to the bookies to back them.

What kills a boss when he gets a sick note is the way in which it is addressed, 'A chara,' when he suspects that this epistle is the work of a cara who is going to leave him in the lurch.

A recent ailment has now superceded all others — the Virus. Viruses have been the greatest Godsend of all time to the medical profession because they cover a multitude and doctors are only too anxious to describe any abstruse symptom as a virus. If a doctor discovers that a fellow is mad he may suggest, 'I think you're suffering from a virus.' The patient is delighted and when he leaves his medical certificate feels like a hand grenade which he is ready to lob in the boss's lap to blow his pretensions to smithereens.

Once a dodger gets a medical cert he is cured instantaneously. He should exercise great care, however, in controlling his elation. Indeed, before resorting to the doctor he should create the impression in the office that he is the most miserable person who ever lived, dying on his feet, etc., so that Boss will insist that he go home. Having made a conspirator of the boss to his little scheme he should proceed homewards at a snail's pace, punctuating his retiral with salvoes of coughing or wheezing like a wounded bagpipes. When he is well clear of the office it is not at all harmful to dance a jig or to emit a few blood-curdling yells which may frighten old women and create a legend locally that the Sioux are on the warpath again.

A gift for making faces is a decided asset on one's return from sick leave. The lugubrious countenance on these occasions is worth any money. It usually elicits such unsolicited remarks as, 'You feeling O.K.?' At this point the good actor comes into his own. One must pooh-pooh the whole affair as if it were nothing while at the same time making every effort to look twice as lugubrious as before. Ten chances to one the word will circulate around the office about how poorly you look or how noble and magnanimous it is of you to report for work in such an awful condition, how you almost fainted or how you refused your morning coffee (even though your tongue was hanging out for it). If your boss is any good (and he cannot afford to risk the displeasure of the ladies with whom you are a firm favourite) he will do the right thing and insist that you go home at once.

Another good technique is to let on that you are crippled with pain. Slit your eyes, grip your hands tightly, make your teeth chatter and draw on the extensive repertoire of facial contortions accumulated so painstakingly over the years. Don't overdo it of course. Have pity on your poor boss. He will be so upset, really sick while you will only be letting on. You don't want to have it on your conscience if he gets a stroke.

This is the type of role you could really enjoy once you don't overdo it for you could break out in a rash or give yourself a real cold.

The sad thing about it all is that if an actor gave such a performance in a film he would, without doubt, be nominated for an Academy Award. It is but a small recompence, therefore, to be nominated by your boss for an extra day off.

If you master the pained look you will be richly rewarded by the number of other pained faces responding to your cue and you may find yourself surrounded by sad-faced people who keep muttering (as much to one another as to you), 'Poor man doesn't look at all well, needs a good tonic, a shame that landlady of his is so callous, etc., etc.' They keep nodding their heads like some kind of clockwork toy, perpetually pouting pained looks at one another. Bloodhounds would be comedians by comparison.

Chalk has been used on occasion to create the ashen look and, of course, soap swallowing is an excellent tonic to induce a fit of frothing and slobbering about the mouth. This should be used only when all other gambits fail as some super-sensitive souls might not want to go on living at the thoughts of the anguish you are going through. Now, see what you've done!

Only once have I met a person who was honest about sick leave. He suffered from angina pectoris and when he returned to the office after a bout would, when asked, 'How are you feeling?' reply, 'Dying, thanks be to God.'

Do not forget bandages, crutches, plaster-casts. Bandages and plaster-casts are great for drawing sympathy. A blood-stained bandage is worth any money. One could be genuinely a nervous wreck without winning an iota of commiseration while a chap with a blood-stained bandage could have women swooning over him.

I once knew a student who kept his perfectly sound arm in a plaster cast all summer long just so long as he would not have to sit an exam for which he had not prepared. So, instead of being soundly berated by his parents they were full of sympathy. The weight of the plaster cast was but a small price to pay for his exemption.

A colleague of mine who was anxious to go to the Listowel Races after his annual leave had been exhausted went to a doctor instead, who asked him to enumerate his symptoms.

'Earache, headache, faceache, legache, no energy, severe pains, depression, tummy upset, swollen tongue, ulcerated gums, rubber legs, palpitations, glands . . .'

'You're a bit off colour,' the doctor interrupted, recognising the litany. 'What you need is a good win at the horses and a holiday in Ballybunion.'

Another was advised by a doctor that if he did not give up smoking he would be dead in a year. 'And if I do give them up, doc,' he said, 'I'll be dead in a week.'

But I digress. Remember, a boss is sick to the gills of common or garden excuses. Take him on a trip with some exotic ailment and even if he does not believe you he'll be grateful because you will have given him something unusual to tell his wife, who may observe that you are a daring fellow. How about Corpuscular kidney disease or homo-globens connubulum for starters?

Let this be your guide then: dispel from your mind the distraught faces of worried taxpayers — it's a lovely sunny day and you want to sample the open spaces instead of fingering through official documents. Dig into your bag of tricks for your finest excuse, one that your boss may safely purloin for his own use in the future for what are bosses but rank and file once or twice removed.

Filling an
Income Tax Form

Every member of the public is absolutely convinced that each civil servant is connected with
income tax and that every form received, for the
purpose of being filled in, will eventually reach
the income tax people. That is why some people
do not fill in social welfare and other miscellaneous
forms; they are afraid that these are all part of a
plot devised by the Revenue Commissioners to
rope them in.

The two most potent words in the English
language next to 'sex appeal,' are 'income tax.'
These two words condition the mind for the
defensive role which must follow the receipt of an
income tax form. If you are a person who does
not like to be boxed in, and what one of us does,
the little rectangular boxes on the form in which
you are required to place your answer, antagonise
you. You think about and resent the neat, unimaginative, statistical mind which devised them
for trapping you. It's bad enough having to pay

income tax without having one's replies confined in rectangles. You feel like a showjumper who has been trained to land in the middle of the box or he will lose marks. If your answers were allowed to overflow the boxes, so to speak, to ramble a bit and be indistinct so that an '8' might resemble an '0' in your favour it would not be so bad. You're paying enough to be allowed this mini-privilege of putting your reply outside a box if you feel so inclined. Of course, rebels will not place their replies in boxes anyway.

Take the section which refers to widowed mothers and other relations unfit to work because of old age or ill health. There are so many intimate details to be filled in and your poor old relative could be harassed to such an extent that it is not worth claiming under this heading for all the harassment and embarassment you are drawing on yourself and those you love. It is indicative of the type of mentality that designed income tax forms in the first place that you are placed in such an invidious position.

Recently I heard a story about decentralisation and mixing with the locals, etc. A crowd of locals were in a pub in the West of Ireland when a whisper began to circulate that the tall bushy-haired man in grey was an income tax man. If the publican had employed him to be on the premises at closing time each night it would have been the most

74

effective way of clearing the premises if one were to judge by the mass exodus of drinkers which followed the disclosure of his occupation.

There is no other form which has ever been designed which causes more heartache, headache, bellyache and intake. People tend to get into a panic at first as if the income tax man were standing behind them, waiting for them to make a false move. Some people don't bother with the boxes — they cramp the auld style, do you know — for they like to range all over the form, telling the assessor what they think of him.

Take the Claim for Personal Allowances: 'If Single' — 'If Married,' — 'If a widower or widow.' A chap with a chip on his shoulder will make the taxman's job harder by stating that he is single but claiming for three mistresses and may even reveal more intimate details if he thinks it could embarass you know who.

Before you start filling an income tax form you have to have scores of other forms before you as well to say nothing of certificates of interest, details of insurance policies, expenses, mortgages, etc. in short, all your dirty washing exposed for their titillation. (It seems that the form is designed in such a way so that replies to questions will supply the taxman with a perennial source of amusement as a small non-monetary stipend for his great work in taking your last bloody penny.)

Who is to say that the information you supplied last year and the year before may not be used in evidence against you this year? (What did you put down last year? Thought so. You'll keep a copy the next time, I'll wager.)

Most salary sections pencil in the amount you earned last year at the top of the form. You will be amazed to discover that on paper at any rate you are a rich man and chagrined to perceive that this lucrative figure appears to have no connection with what goes into your pocket. The income tax man is the middleman and did you ever hear tell of a middleman who lost out on any racket?

You are sorely tempted to concoct a few relatives. More power to you if you get away with it. But tell me this, would the invention of two mothers-in-law be compensated for by the extra allowances in the event of their materialising?

You are always afraid that you did not claim enough and that money to which you are rightfully entitled is piling up to the credit of the Revenue Commissioners. When hard-up your thoughts dwell constantly on this money. You hope that when you least expect it a fine fat cheque will be pushed through your letter box.

Income tax men have a genius for splitting hairs. You think perhaps that you are entitled to full exemption in respect of some particular deduction only to discover that because of some obsolete law you are only entitled to a fraction of it — to wit, 323 ÷ 999. This is pure genius, guaranteed to increase heart attacks and create vacancies for school leavers at a time when jobs are scarce.

An income tax form, at the very best of times, is a formidable document and once you have filled it in and it has left your premises you may spend the rest of the year regretting your impetuosity because it can make you or break you. There should be some incentive for filling in all the 'Nones' one is obliged to fill in. If a colleague asks you what you earn say to him, 'I'll tell you how much income tax I pay, instead.' It is a much better status symbol.

Man's natural inclination to boast receives a severe jolt. Boasting on a tax form can be a costly exercise. There is a mathematical formula which determines what one tells wife or friends about one's intake of pints; when you're telling the lads, multiply and when you're telling the wife, divide. The income tax man should be included with the distaff side.

But cheer up. There's so much pressure being exerted now on successive governments that income tax is bound to go one of these days and in the expectation that we are about to enter Shangri-La I leave you to count your coppers.

On Looking into Empty Envelopes

Every morning in the registry of a large office when the post is received a conscientious officer will look into an envelope after the contents have been removed to ensure that no further correspondence remains within. Some over-cautious types, akin to those who go downstairs several times each night to ensure that they have switched off the electricity or locked the back door, may look into the envelope several times.

I once knew a person for whom this chore became an obsession and half of her official life was spent staring into empty envelopes. The envelope became her escape hatch, her retreat. It was not unusual to discover her standing — legs apart and arms outstretched — with the fingers of each hand ribbing the inside of the envelope so that she could more effectively crane her head into it. Sometimes she would hold the envelope waist high whilst she stared downwards into its recesses and at other times it would be raised above her head whilst she peered aloft, presumably in the expectation of having a torrent of documents pour over her.

She had a particular liking for raising foolscap size envelopes above her head and seen in this position she resembled a female bishop about to don her mitre for the first time. Her eyes became glazed, her rotund body settled more firmly on her squat legs as she gazed fixedly at the opening. It took the concentrated efforts of several elbows to prod her back into reality.

In spite of this double-barrelled dedication it was a regrettable fact that correspondence was frequently found in envelopes which she had thus scrutinised.

Of course, she was completely unaware that she suffered from a fixation but it was noticeable that subsequent to a peeping session she seemed remarkably refreshed as if indeed she had imbibed from the fountain of youth. In her case, the habit had the effect of relaxing her although, unfortunately, it seemed to have the opposite effect on her boss who was responsible for the accuracy of her work.

Her affliction became so acute that she affected every young girl in the office to a greater or lesser degree with a minor form of this disease as a result of which scarcely anyone recruited in a part-time capacity to this job was able to fight the irresistible urge to peep into an envelope.

A young person might remove the contents and throw away the envelope only to have second thoughts moments later. It was not an unusual sight to see normally calm young ladies up to their oxters in discarded envelopes, rummaging for the elusive one they felt might still contain buried treasure.

The envelope-peeper had the duty also of recording the whereabouts of particular files in a register specifically designed for that purpose. It was a job which should have taken approximately forty minutes daily to complete but in the hands of the lady with the fixation it took hours on end. She was a bad case of contagious uncertainty, which disease spreads with the rapidity of a prairie fire.

For instance, she would place a file beside her on her desk, having first removed it from its envelope, observe that it had been marked to, say, a Mr O'Sullivan, extract the appropriate register and mark the file in to Head Office. She would then forget that she had done so, extract the register again and re-mark the file to a totally different destination. This practice might go on and on until the file was simultaneously marked to several different places. It did not help her concentration to be interrupted at regular intervals by an elderly gentleman who worked opposite her. When he was under the influence, and he seldom was under any other influence, he felt the need to unburden himself of the many fallacious theories his drink-sodden brain prompted. He might speak of the number of bricks laid hourly by Russian bricklayers or he might refer to the number of flies trampled by the feet of those who danced on the grape to make wine. She would sit with her eyes rivetted to his face, waiting with her own anecdote on the tip of her tongue for a pause but he had a sense of acceleration that would leave a jaguar in the shade and the poor woman became so frustrated that she did not know whether she was coming or going. Work was either at a standstill during these disclosures or else was so inaccurately accomplished that it would have been better for her section if she had been seized with writer's cramp.

Thus, files which were incoming would, when the register was referred to, reveal themselves to be outgoing and files which a Mr Andrews would assure everybody that he had penned to a Mr Pettigrew would stand marked to a Mr McGillicuddy and a score of other outdoor officers. Some of these files were never traced, so elusive was their itinerary.

Eventually, in the interests of reliability, her boss, who could not get rid of her, gave her the job which she was assuredly born for: that of ensuring that all contents had been removed from empty envelopes which occupation she may still be engaged in, for all I know.

Contagious Confusion

In my chapter on the subject of Looking into Empty Envelopes I referred to contagious uncertainty. I now wish to refer to its natural consequence — contagious confusion.

Envelope-peepers, clerks with a double and treble-checking complex and those who devote the entire pigeon-holing resources of an office to filing useless pieces of information create an ideal climate for the spread of contagious confusion.

In this state not alone is a particular person not sure of anything but he or she, by example, may afflict his or her companions in a similar way so that no one can say at any given moment whether a situation which should be self-evident is or is not as it should be. Contagious confusion is like the flu. It spreads rapidly and the only way to cure it is to isolate those who are worst affected until such time as things return to normal.

I remember one particular section of a certain office whose staff suffered from more than their fair share of contagious confusion, where every routine job was approached with contagious uncertainty. As a consequence ink was spilled (people used ink in offices once upon a time), files were mislaid (some to the eternal gratification of bosses) never to be found again; incorrect decisions were taken, then reversed; wrong entries were made then regretted, affirmatives turned into shoddy negatives and buckpassers passed more bucks than they received.

But it is in the immediate aftermath of the receipt of a thorny question that contagious uncertainty and subsequently contagious confusion come into their own.

For example, a directive is issued. If it is written it may be badly-worded or if it is verbal it may be that it is not clear to everybody what information exactly it is that is required. Rather than make the necessary enquiries some higher official goes off half-cocked and half the staff are put to work digging out information. It may be something like this: How many male or female creditors live within a radius of twenty-five miles of Dublin and how many live within a radius of sixty miles? It may be a question whose relevance to anything is not particularly clear but the directive in connection with it, for one reason or another, is misinterpreted and so begins the uncertainty which inevitably leads to the subsequen con-fusion. Vagueness is the perfect climate for the fermentation of contagious uncertainty. If a boss-man is asked if a certain premise is so and when, not being sure, he replies in the affirmative he has set a chain of events in motion which causes many headaches, heart-searchings, wild goose chases, merry-go-rounds and replies which do not measure up to expectations.

Working under a cloud of contagious confusion is like having a perpetual sword of Damocles hovering over one's head. There is the constant fear of the necessity for changing horses in mid-stream.

I once knew an old lady on a ten year extension of service who was hopelessly inadequate in the hurly-burly of a busy office. Sometimes people such as she were retained in a sort of permanent temporary capacity by reason of influence, or pull as it is commonly referred to. This particular old lady might be given the job of putting filing cards with six digit numbers, already in third figure order, into strict order and the end result would be, after her efforts, that they would be in complete disorder. During the course of this operation she would have nodded off to sleep several times or in the seclusion of the women's cloakroom would have taken a swig or two from the baby whiskey which was suspended from a chain around her neck but not visible to the casual observer.

It was a blessing when she fell asleep because someone else could then do her job. It was not so easy to persuade her when she awoke that she had completed it before she had nodded off. She suspected a conspiracy from the acquiescent smiles on the faces of her colleagues. She took umbrage if her boss suggested she take a rest and let someone else finish her work. Her toothless jaws worked up and down in aggrievement, making her say, 'I suppose you think I am not able for it.' When she was assured that everyone thought the complete opposite she grudgingly allowed herself to be persuaded.

Another person used to request a document from a store in the basement on an official form specially designed therefor. Official request forms were in two parts, one part divided from the other by perforated lines. The top portion of this form was for requests and the bottom was for accompanying the document back to the person who requested it. When the document was forwarded to a particular clerk by the paper keeper he retained the top portion and forwarded the bottom half with the document to her. When this document was subsequently returned to him he withdrew the official request form (top portion) from its filing sequence and re-inserted the document in its place. The top portion of the official request form, being no longer relevant, was then scrapped.

Not so with the clerk at the other end. When she returned the document to the paper keeper her bottom half of the official form was of no further use and should have been scrapped but she retained all these useless pieces of paper and in over twenty years of requesting documents she had acquired a whole pigeon-holed room full of them. So she managed to justify her existence by continually referring to and constantly re-filing these parts of official request forms which long ago ceased to have any relevance to anything but added another layer to the mountain of confusion which daily grew by the efforts of people such as herself. O x M was still a long way off.

The Art of Ducking

If one hopes to survive in this world without getting a stroke or going mad as a result of frustration one must be a ducker of the first order. Skipping, evasion and side-stepping are only second cousins of ducking which is a scientific art, brought to its peak during the last war by small-town drinkers who had to contend not only with their wives but also with the Civic Guards as they ducked in and out of pubs.

The small town in which I grew up was honeycombed with backways and back alleys. Across the road from our house there was an archway which led into an intricate labyrinth of backlanes. There was a public house on either side of this archway. Customers, in bad odour with their wives, had a readymade escape route. Similar archways appeared in other streets so that one might say that there were two thoroughfares. One was for those who could go openly about their business such as old ladies wheeling prams, painters, sign writers and divines. Behind the scenes, as it were, the real life of the town existed where the dodgers and duckers of everyday life reacted to the sight of petticoat or policeman.

If you ever hear a woman say, 'He was a right ducker,' you know that you are hearing of the exploits of a master dodger, a quick thinker and an even quicker drinker who broke her bloody heart.

A ducker has to possess the skill and coolness in the face of danger of a matador. He must have superb body control, the twirling toes of a ballet dancer and the daring swerve of a fencer.

A mind for a pint, an inability to make a decision, a failure to take life seriously, a desire to escape, a penchant for going against the grain — these are but a few of the incentives which inspire a ducker. A ducker wants to duck his wife (on payday), his boss whenever he can, a Civic Guard, a process server, an income tax inspector or someone he diddled and above all, his responsibilities.

A born ducker must duck. He would be untrue to his calling if he did not. Seeking to watch a ducker in action is almost as difficult as trying to spot a leprechaun hiding his crock of gold.

Ducking only comes into its own in such places as building sites, department stores, airports, railway stations and government offices with large floor space where there are escalators, dual stairways, lifts and secret passageways.

Many of the progeny of small town duckers now put their inherited skills to the test in lifts or on the dual stairways of government offices. They will match their skills with city duckers who have mastered their trade in cramped bookies' offices, on the spiral staircases of multi-storeyed flats and in pubs.

Next to a mad bull there is nothing as frustrated and dangerous as a thwarted ducker. That is why many duckers escape out of prison. Confinement inspires their ingenuity in seeking means to escape.

Frequently your daring ducker will rub shoulders with the person he wishes to duck. This gambit adds spice to the ducking. Often the best hiding place is under the other fellow's nose where he least expects to find you. There is a great thrill in standing next to your boss in a bookie's joint. He is absentmindedly picking winners and proffers you a light on request without realising who you are and without displaying an iota of interest in you. This is the ultimate in ducking, as thrilling as Russian Roulette. If he backs a loser he will be on to you like a shot and your reflexes must be razor sharp to enable you to employ the double skip, slip, wiggle and riggle.

A ducker has to show his hand to a certain extent to win the acclaim of his colleagues. Working in close confines he is not too concerned once he ducks the person he is trying to duck whether or not he leaves a trail for lesser mortals to follow. Thus only, in such circumstances, has it been possible to record and classify the many diverse ducks of a ducker.

A ducker is never without his newspaper for a newspaper is one of the best and most natural shields ever invented. A ducker would not dream of reading his paper. He is too busy doing the dance of the seven veils behind it. Umbrellas are not bad either. There is nothing as bewildering as a piece of umbrella-twirling magic.

On Saturday morning a five-day week ducker expects a rest but he may be stuck with taking the kids to confession where he has the task of ducking the clergy or the do-gooders who would rope him into their pious schemes. Or he may be stuck with the shopping list when he knows he already used the housekeeping money to back horses. In ducking with deceit one has to co-ordinate mental and physical ducking in order to remain one step ahead of the posse.

Women love a good ducker even though he may be ducking them. They admire his technique. Personally I have always believed that there should be a Faculty of Ducking at the Universities although it is already practised by the highest in the land who might be called gifted amateur duckers. You have all heard of Grand National duckers — jockeys who sat their horses in the mist and only did one round.

Ducking and dodging the issue are blood brothers. It is possible, if one is a skilful ducker, to avoid ever having to make a decision. It helps to pass forty odd years, if one is a civil servant for instance, before one goes out on pension to a more restricted type of ducking.

There are many duckers in the Dail and reverend duckers surprise people by turning up in pubs where all true duckers eventually gravitate to duck for a little while longer before they inevitably descend into the aperture from which, alas, there is no escape.

What finer epitaph to have on one's tomb than the simple words, 'Here lies a Ducker!'

MORE MERCIER BESTSELLERS

THE BOOK OF KERRYMAN JOKES
Des MacHale

How do you recognise a Kerryman on an oil rig?
He's the one throwing crusts of bread to the helicopters.

****

What's an oscillator?
A Kerryman who eats donkeys.

ENGLISHMAN JOKES FOR IRISHMEN
Des MacHale

What do you call an Englishman with an I.Q. of 50?
Colonel Sir!

****

How do you recognise an insulation conscious upper class Englishman?
He's got double glazing in his monocle.

LETTERS OF A SUCCESSFUL T.D.
John B. Keane
This bestseller takes a humourous peep at the correspondence of an Irish parliamentary deputy.

LETTERS OF AN IRISH PARISH PRIEST
John B. Keane
There is a riot of laughter in every page and its theme is the correspondence between a country parish priest and his nephew who is studying to be a priest.

LETTERS OF AN IRISH PUBLICAN
John B. Keane

One of Ireland's most popular humourous authors shows us the life of a small Irish town as seen through the eyes of the local publican.

THE GENTLE ART OF MATCHMAKING and other important things
John B. Keane

An amusing collection of short essays by Ireland's most prolific writer and playwright.

LETTERS OF A LOVE-HUNGRY FARMER
John B. Keane

John B. Keane has introduced a new word into the English language — *chastitute*. This is the story of a cchastitute, i.e. a man who has never lain down with a woman ifor reasons which are fully disclosed within this book. It is the tale of a lonely man who will not humble himself to achieve his heart's desire, whose need for female companionship whines and whimpers throughout. Here are the hilarious sex escapades of John Bosco McLane culminating finally in one dreadful deed.

LETTERS OF A COUNTRY POSTMAN
John B. Keane

A hilarious account of the exploits of a postman in rural Ireland.

LETTERS OF A MATCHMAKER
John B. Keane

Comparisons may be odious but the readers will find it fascinating to contrast the Irish matchmaking system with that of the 'Cumangettum Love Parlour' in Philadelphia. They will meet many unique characters from the Judas Jennies of New York to Fionnuala Crust of Coomasahara who buried two giant-sized, sexless husbands but eventually found happiness with a pint-sized jockey from north Cork.

LETTERS OF A CIVIC GUARD
John B. Keane

Garda Leo Molair's role is one which has been created by follies and weaknesses of his fellows. Consequently folly and weakness dominate the greater part of the correspondence of this book.

IS THE HOLY GHOST REALLY A KERRYMAN?
(And other topics of interest)
John B. Keane

Is the Holy Ghost really a Kerryman? The obvious answer to that is: if he is not a Kerryman what is he? Is he just another ghost, a mere figment of the imagination like Hamlet's father, or is he something more sinister: a Corkman masquerading as a Kerryman or worse still a real Kerryman but having an inferiority complex; that is to say a Kerryman who thinks he's only the same as everybody else?

Following the phenomenal success of John B. Keane's books, who can resist Keane on such varied topics as 'Wakes', 'Streaking', 'Epitaphs' and 'Long-Distance Talkers'? Nobody should miss reading this hilariously funny and entertaining book.

STRONG TEA
John B. Keane

A selection of pin-pointing articles and stories from the pen of John B. Keane. Tickling the traits of our neighbours, John B. sees in the everyday actions of those around us a wealth of humour and wisdom.

THE COMIC HISTORY OF IRELAND
E.J. Delaney and J.M. Feehan

History of the variety which you will find in the pregnant pages of this book is not manufactured on the battle fronts of a war-torn world, it is gouged out with the sweat and blood and blots and even tears, in the heat of many a hard-fought examination.